Heartlifting
Blessings to

_____

In celebration of who you are
and the triumphant way you live your life

What a Joy It Is to Know You,

_____

_____

date

Surprising Stories, Stirring Messages, and
Refreshing Scriptures That Make the Heart Soar

heartlifters™

for the *young* at *heart*

Susan Duke

Personalized Scriptures by
LeAnn Weiss

HOWARD
PUBLISHING CO.

Special foldout pages

Our purpose at Howard Publishing is to:

- *Increase faith* in the hearts of growing
  Christians
- *Inspire holiness* in the lives of believers
- *Instill hope* in the hearts of struggling people
  everywhere

Because He's coming again!

Heartlifters™ for the Young at Heart © 2001 by Susan Duke
All rights reserved. Printed in Hong Kong
Published by Howard Publishing Co., Inc.
3117 North 7th Street, West Monroe, Louisiana 71291-2227

01 02 03 04 05 06 07 08 09 10   10 9 8 7 6 5 4 3 2 1

Personalized scriptures by LeAnn Weiss, owner of Encouragement Company
3006 Brandywine Dr., Orlando, FL 32806; (407) 898-4410

Edited by Bob Kelly
Interior design by Stephanie Denney

Library of Congress Cataloging-in-Publication Data
Duke, Susan.
    Heartlifters for the young at heart : surprising stories, stirring messages, and refreshing
scriptures that make the heart soar / Susan Duke ; personalized scriptures by LeAnn Weiss.
        p. cm.
    ISBN 1-58229-157-8
    1. Christian aged—Religious life. I. Weiss, LeAnn. II. Title.
    BV4580 .D85 2001
    242'.65—dc21

                                                                      00-053892

Scripture quotations are from The Holy Bible, Authorized King James Version, © 1961 by The
National Publishing Co.

CONTENTS

CONTENTS

INSIGHT

Anna Mary Robertson's career as a painter didn't begin until her seventieth birthday—and then almost by accident—when her younger sister coaxed her into trying to use a paintbrush.

Arthritis had made it difficult to do the fancy needlework she'd learned at age twelve while working as a "hired girl" for a well-to-do family—the Whitesides. Mrs. Whiteside taught Anna to make the "prettiest fancy work in Washington County."

But Anna was more intrigued by the pictures that hung in the White-side home, and she began studying and drawing them after Mr. Whiteside gave her the first chalk crayons she'd ever seen. The scenes reminded her of how her father had raised her to soak up the simple beauty of the land that surrounded her. "A body can't daydream indoors, must have earth and sky for dreaming and being blessed with second sight," he said.

Anna worked in several homes before she married at age twenty-seven. She bore ten children—half of whom she buried in infancy.

INSIGHT

> *It is never too late to be what you might have been.*
>
> —GEORGE ELIOT

At age seventy-five, Anna bought her first real artist's brushes and "oil paint in tubes" at W. D. Thomas's drugstore. Four years later she priced four paintings at two dollars each and hung them in the drugstore window. A part-time art collector, Mr. Louis J. Caldor, bought all four paintings and asked how to find Anna.

"He was the snowball that started the avalanche," Anna recalled years later. He persuaded Mr. Otto Kallir, a world-renowned art authority, to look at her work and sponsor Anna's first "showing."

During World War II, her paintings were sent overseas and were viewed by more than one hundred thousand people. "The world," in Emerson's words, "beat a path to her door." Anna, known around the world as Grandma Moses, had never set foot in art school but had received all the awards they had to offer.

2

INSIGHT

When Anna was eighty-nine, President Harry S. Truman presented her with the Women's National Press Club's Achievement Award for outstanding accomplishment in art.

New York governor Nelson Rockefeller declared September 7, 1961 "Grandma Moses Day," proclaiming, "Her lesson of life will last as long as her pictures. For the old she left the lesson of renewed spirit and zest for life—that dawn's brightest colors can be saved to give twilight its glow. To the young—she left the lesson of her life—by which she has stimulated and inspired a yearning for a simplicity that brings contentment to walking the earth and a kinship with nature that gives security to the walk."

Anna's painting titled *July 4* was presented to the American people and still hangs in the White House. Before she died at the age of 101, Grandma Moses had painted more than sixteen hundred pictures and taken her place among the great artists of the world. Her paintings now hang in museums across the country. But perhaps her greatest legacy was expressed by her son who said, "She taught us to make good tracks."

Have you ever stood and gazed at a sunset? I don't mean gazed in the sense that you noticed or casually observed it. But have you ever truly allowed yourself to be caught up in the wonder of God's magnificent handiwork—marveled at His suspended curtain—brilliantly displayed with opalescent swirls of orange and purple hues against a sapphire blue sky?

Observation and insight are wonderful attributes that give your eyes "heart" and permit them to contemplate majesty and simplicity at the same time.

Insight connects you to the wonderment within your soul.

Responsibilities and challenges of life can easily steal your joy if you're not careful. But God uses nature to paint a picture bigger than your life—to give you a broader focus. Just as you look for the "meaning" in paintings by the old art masters, the Master Artist wants you to find His meaning in the painting He has created just for you! Look and see! Observe. Think. Delight in the little things that often go unnoticed in your hurried schedule.

Take time to "smell the roses." Bask in the fragrance of His heavenly bounty! Listen for His voice in the gentle breeze or rippling brook, and hear your heart speak through a crimson sunset. Unearth the treasure of bliss you knew as a child when your eyes were keen with expectation.

Insightful living will rekindle your senses, refresh your spirit, and open your eyes to everyday miracles waiting to be painted upon the canvas of your life.

INSIGHT

Always remember that I am your eternal fountain of life. Nothing compares to the surpassing greatness of knowing Me. In My light, you gain understanding. May your love grow in knowledge and depth of insight so that you'll be able to choose My best, becoming pure and blameless until the day of Christ. Don't forget that you're a reflection of Me and that I'm transforming you into My likeness with an ever-increasing glory!

Shining on you,

*Your God
of Wisdom*

Psalm 36:9
Philippians 3:8; 1:9–10
2 Corinthians 3:18

I am your eternal fountain of life…

GRACIOUSNESS

At age seventy-two, Fred rises each day at 5:00 A.M. to read the Bible, write letters, and swim at a nearby club. There is no desk, telephone, or computer in his office, but there are cherished mementos of those who have loved him into existence through the years.

He still writes in longhand on a yellow legal pad every episode of his almost nine hundred (to date) programs, and each episode is dedicated to his mission of broadcasting "grace" throughout the land.

During childhood Fred dreamed of becoming a pastor. But in later years, when he came home to Latrobe, Pennsylvania, for a weekend visit from college, he saw his parents' television and changed his mind—realizing how many people this medium could reach.

After college graduation in 1951, Fred moved to New York to work in television. He married Joanne—a girl he'd met in college—returned to Pennsylvania in 1953, and helped launch the first community-supported public television station in the country.

Before his first program aired,

The evening of the year brings with it its lamp.

—JOSEPH JOUBERT

producer Dorothy Daniel held a party to celebrate the new show (complete with party favors). He used the favor he'd received (a tiger puppet) on the first episode of *The Children's Corner*. It was such a hit that Fred began using other puppets and voices for the show's characters.

In 1954, Fred enrolled in seminary. For eight years he went to classes during lunch breaks, hoping to fulfill his desire to create programs for the church. The day before receiving his diploma, denominational officials canceled financial support of Fred's planned television program due to lack of funds.

Thinking the program was God's avenue for his ministry, Fred was disappointed. But the following day, he received a call from Canada to develop a new program that featured him—in addition to his puppets.

After working in Canada for a year, he returned to

Pittsburgh knowing exactly what kind of ministry God had called him to. His new show aired locally for two years but was loved by so many children that stations all over the country wanted it. In 1968, his program went national.

Fred describes his calling as an advocate for children, stating that "they always need to know that they are loved and capable of loving." Ordained by the Presbyterian church as an "evangelist to work with children and families through the mass media," he is known the world over from his program of thirty-two years, *Mister Rogers' Neighborhood*—public television's longest-running show.

"Every time I walk into the studio, I pray, 'Let some word that is heard be Yours.' The Holy Spirit translates our best efforts into what needs to be communicated to that person in his or her place of need."

Having received every major television award, Fred Rogers still believes that those in television "are chosen to be servants to help meet deeper needs." His example of graciousness and what he calls "loving someone into existence" continue to set a time-honored standard for all ages.

Remember the good ol' days? If you're like me, when you hear that question, your heart smiles, you sigh, and a movie reel of memories begins playing in your mind.

You remember…the days before computers, fax machines, answering machines, and pagers. Days when you could still borrow sugar from a neighbor and stay long enough for a porch-swing visit or spend a lazy summer afternoon playing checkers with a friend.

Simpler times. Before road rage and Internet highways. Blissful times—when Sunday dinner was almost as special as the church service. Or when hunting for four-leaf clovers, playing hopscotch, and finding pictures in puffy white clouds kept you happy by day—and stargazing beneath luminous skies soothed your soul at night.

Sitting on the ice-cream freezer while a little bit of heaven on earth was being cranked out meant you were important to a very special event—family time. Those were the days when graciousness was as natural as breathing and people defined their lives by its meaning: grace, politeness, courtesy, kindness, respect, and friendliness.

By remembering yesterday's simple joys and extending a cup of old-fashioned graciousness to others, you

help keep the spirit of the good ol' days alive forever!
Someone once said, "People may not remember what
you did or said, but they'll always remember how you
made them feel."

So despite the world's condition, each time you
bake some "just because" cookies to share with your
neighbor, read a story to a child, or bend down to eye
level and say "You're special," you keep the candle of
yesteryear burning brightly and pass the legacy of graciousness to another generation.

I am compassionate and gracious, slow to anger, and abounding in love for you. My compassions for you never fail; they are new and available for you each and every morning. Because of My love for you, I didn't even spare Jesus. You can trust Me to graciously give you all things.

Graciously,

Your Loving God

Psalm 103:8; Lamentations 3:22–23
Romans 8:32

I am compassionate and gracious…

FAITHFULNESS

After being raised and trained by her father to carry on the family's one-hundred-year-old watchmaking business, in 1918 Cornelia became the first licensed female watchmaker in Holland.

But at age fifty, Cornelia found herself in the middle of a national crisis that changed her life forever. Faced with the question of what part she would play in helping her war-ravaged country, she prayed, "Lord Jesus, I offer myself for your people. In any way. Any place. Any time."

Within days of Cornelia's prayer, her entire family became a vital part of an underground rescue mission by hiding all who came to their house seeking refuge from racial persecution.

In February 1944, after a trusted friend betrayed Cornelia's family and told the Gestapo of their activities, they were all arrested for harboring fugitive Jews. While imprisoned in Ravensbruck Concentration Camp, Cornelia and her sister Betsy smuggled in Bibles, translated the Dutch Bible into German, and ministered to their

In the end, it's not the years in your life that count. It's the life in your years.

—ABRAHAM LINCOLN

fellow inmates who gathered to hear God's Word. They even thanked God for the fleas that kept the guards away from their dormitory, allowing them to minister without hindrance.

Cornelia experienced the loss of her father, her sister Betsy, and a nephew while in the concentration camp. She was released in 1945 by mistake due to a clerical error and later learned that one week after her release, all other women her age had been executed in the gas chambers. "I knew my life had been given back for a purpose…I was no longer my own."

In 1945, Cornelia set up a ministry in Bloemendaal for the war-damaged people of Holland. Despite the horror and pain she suffered, Cornelia remained faithful, not only to God, but to people who needed His love.

She later opened her own father's house and renovated a German concentration camp for refugees. She eventually traveled to more than sixty countries sharing the message of God's restoration and love and her message that "there is no pit too deep that Jesus is not deeper still."

When she was seventy-five years old, Cornelia, known worldwide as Corrie ten Boom, did not let injuries from a serious car wreck slow her down. She helped speed her recovery by working with weights and exercising her fingers through playing the piano, and she taught herself to write left-handed.

Corrie ten Boom's faithfulness to her mission only increased as she grew older. She published eighteen books, totaling more than six million copies sold. *The Hiding Place* sold more than a million copies and became a movie seen by more than fifteen million people.

Until her death in 1983, Corrie ten Boom remained faithful to her and her sister's dream of telling the world, "that when the worst happens in the life of a child of God, the best remains."

Mountain climbers believe they can climb mountains and actually reach the summit—or they'd never gather their supplies and start climbing. Even the endurance and perseverance of seasoned climbers are challenged with each new ascent.

What keeps them climbing, often in perilous weather, is the faith that they're able to scale the heights. The reward for all their labor? The fulfillment of connecting to something grand—something bigger than themselves—and the breathtakingly beautiful view from the top!

FAITH

Do you realize that you're a mountain climber? Each day God equips you with all you need to scale the heights of every mountain in your life. With every small slope of circumstance or prodigious challenge you conquer, you build faith muscles, strengthening you for the next climb!

There may be moments when mist or fog blocks the glorious view of victory—and at times you may wonder if you can keep climbing—but God is on every rocky ledge, reaching out to guide you to greater heights of faith.

21

Paul didn't know what might befall him in Jerusalem but declared he was still going—compelled by the convictions of his own spirit (Acts 20:22). He proclaimed that his trust in God was greater than any impending danger when he said, "But none of these things move me!" (v. 24).

Faithfulness is immovable trust! It's not something you do but who you are. Faithfulness seeks God's light in the darkness—with steadfast assurance that He is working out all things for your good—and takes you from glory to glory to the peaks of wondrous victory.

I preserve you when you're faithful. Your faith is more valuable than gold and is refined through testing. Even your smallest seed of faith has mountain-moving capability. My faithfulness was established in heaven itself, and you can be totally confident that I will complete the good work I started in you. May you finish strong, abiding in faith all the days of your life.

Faithfully through all generations,

Your God

Psalm 31:23; Matthew 17:20
1 Peter 1:7; Psalm 89:2
Philippians 1:6
2 Timothy 4:7

*I will complete the good work
I started in you…*

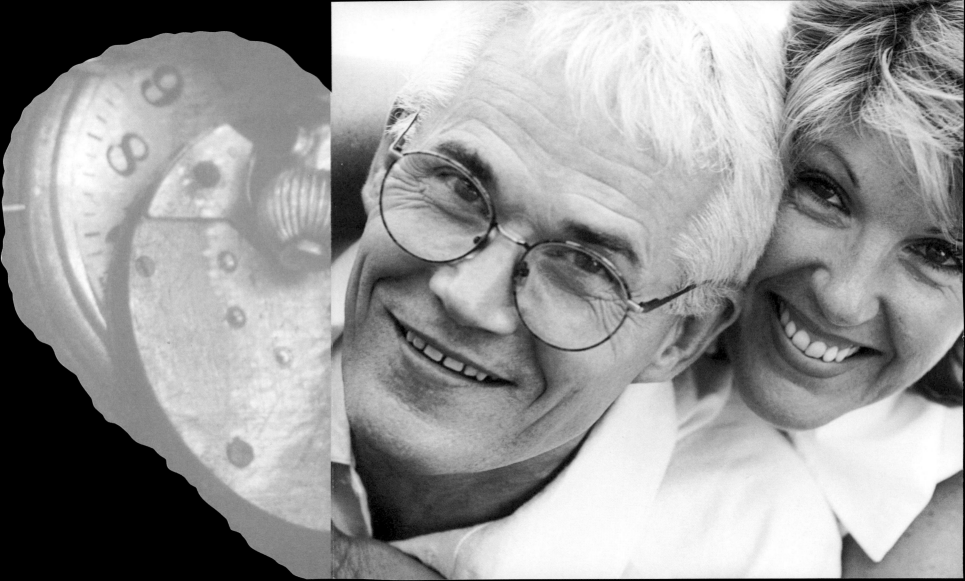

SERVANTHOOD

He was fifty-three years old when he was inaugurated as the thirty-ninth president of the United States. On January 20, 1977, the nation welcomed the honest, old-fashioned ideals brought from his down-to-earth rural Baptist upbringing. Someone jokingly observed that his presidency was used as a steppingstone to higher things.

As a small boy, James carried water to the farmhands, filled the seed planters and fertilizer distributors, and ran errands. Farm life was simple in the close-knit community of Archery, Georgia, where he grew up. His father owned and operated a small country store and a 360-acre farm that produced watermelons, pecans, cotton, sweet potatoes, honey, milk, fruits and vegetables, timber, peanuts, and wool from their sheep.

During the 1930s and 1940s, his father, Earl, branched out into commodities, brokering, and other business ventures.

In 1946, James received a much-desired appointment to the U.S. Naval Academy at Annapolis. In July of the

Lives of great men all remind us that we can make our lives sublime. And, departing, leave behind us footsteps on the sands of time.

—HENRY WADSWORTH LONGFELLOW

same year, he married his sister's best friend. James later served two years on the USS *Pomfret* before being selected to work on the nuclear submarine program.

Following his father's death in 1953, James resigned from the navy and returned to Georgia to take over the family farm. He successfully established himself as a businessman and farmer, became involved in community affairs, and served two terms as a state senator. He ran for governor in 1966 and lost.

After losing that election, James reassessed his life and became a "born-again" Christian, stating, "The presence of my belief in Christ is the most important thing in my life."

He ran for governor again in 1970 and won. He served for four years and decided to run for president.

Jimmy Carter has been called the "the best ex-president the U.S. has had since Herbert Hoover."

26

After leaving office, he's worked tirelessly through his Presidential Library and Carter Center in Atlanta, sponsoring programs promoting human rights, education, agriculture, and healthcare—especially in Third World countries.

He's written eight books, still teaches an adult Sunday school class at the Plains Baptist Church in Georgia, and he and his wife, Rosalynn, spend a week each year building low-income homes through Habitat for Humanity.

He has been the recipient of numerous awards and honorary degrees. In 1999, Carter was awarded the Presidential Medal of Freedom, the nation's highest civilian honor.

At age seventy-seven, an energetic Jimmy Carter enjoys fly-fishing, hunting, and writing books, and he continues to use his unique position to influence events around the world.

The founders of Habitat for Humanity, Linda and Millard Fuller, said of him, "Whether he is swinging a hammer, resolving a conflict, stamping out human rights abuse, lending a helping hand to a neighbor, or teaching Sunday school, it is obvious that Jimmy Carter takes great joy in being a servant of God."

*W*hat if…the only news the media reported was good news? I wonder if there'd be enough praise reports, kindness alerts, and charitable announcements to fill the time slots? Unfortunately, we probably won't get to experience such joyful tidings until we get to heaven.

But suppose every person on earth purposed in their hearts to look for someone to bless each day? Not in extraordinary ways, but in simple ordinary gestures of goodwill. Today's self-centered culture may not see the value in such efforts, but the rewards of blessing others would fill our world with good news!

Servanthood is an exciting and adventurous way of

life. It's the spontaneous, private little tokens of service that develop the heart of a true servant. You and I may not be able to philosophically reform the world at large into a mission field of benevolence, but individually we can make a difference.

It has been said that Jesus had the power of a king but the heart of a servant. The most powerful man who ever walked this earth "made himself of no reputation, but took upon him the form of a servant" (Philippians 2:7). During his time on earth, Jesus went about looking for people to bless!

The next time you go a department or grocery

store, ask God to allow someone to cross your path whom you can bless—and see what happens! Someone today needs your reassuring smile, your words of compassion, encouragement, and validation.

Joy follows hearts that serve. In serving, you become Christ's love extended—using the wellspring of gifts and talents you've been given to bring refreshment to weary souls.

You are a citizen of heaven. So serve in My strength. I enrich your life in every way so you can generously reinvest in others on all occasions. Stand firm, giving yourself fully to My work, knowing that your labor in Me is never unproductive. Follow Me by serving your way to greatness. May you experience vitality and fulfillment even in your senior years.

Humbly,

Jesus

Philippians 3:20; 1 Peter 4:11
2 Corinthians 9:11; 1 Corinthians 15:58
Psalm 92:12–14

I enrich your life in every way…

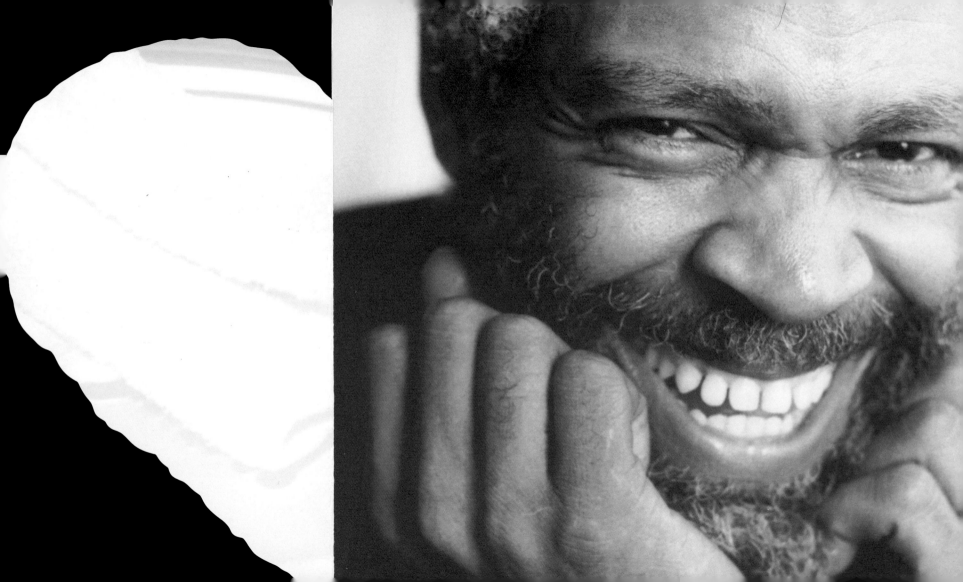

CREATIVITY

Throughout his life, he never lost the nickname Sparky, which was given to him by an uncle when he was born, nor did he forget his kindergarten teacher who recognized his unique talent and proclaimed, "Sparky, someday you will be an artist."

Sparky's artistic passion never waned and seemed to grow even greater in his older years. "It seems beyond comprehension that I was born to draw comic strips, but I think I was," Sparky once said. Drawing from his own childhood, his experiences of raising five children, and the experiences of personal friends, he created a gallery of memorable characters.

Sparky's father owned a barbershop, and during the Depression, he managed to stay in business and even provide money to enroll Sparky in a correspondence art school. Sparky struggled through the program and earned a C+ in "Drawing of Children."

Just after Sparky completed his art course, he was inducted into the military during World War II. Within days

Every artist dips his brush into his own soul, and paints his own nature in his own pictures.

—HENRY WARD BEECHER

of being drafted, his mother, who had battled cancer for seven years, passed away.

Sparky's artistic dreams were put on hold while he was in the service, but when he returned to St. Paul, Minnesota, after his discharge, he was hired to do the lettering for cartoons in a small Roman Catholic magazine.

Sparky took on a second job teaching with Art Instruction Schools and found the support and practice he needed. He eventually sold a number of single cartoon panels to several church publications and later to the *Saturday Evening Post*. His next success came when he landed a weekly comic feature—*L'il Folks* for the *St. Paul Pioneer Press*, which was syndicated nationally. His major breakthrough came when a top United Feature Syndicate editor saw his work, suggested he change his one-panel comic to a strip format, and offered him a five-year contract.

CREATIVITY

Deeply religious, but with a "quiet faith," Sparky used his strip in the beginning to creatively illustrate themes of Christian teaching in subtle and symbolic ways—careful to never be "preachy" or pious. By blending Christianity and real life, he found a way to make religion funny without mockery.

Once readers accepted the classic Peanuts-gang series, which Charles Schulz ("Sparky") brought to life, it became the most successful comic strip in newspaper history, appearing in twenty-six hundred newspapers in seventy-five countries and translated into twenty-six languages. Throughout fifty years of success, the *Peanuts* series has included a thousand books, thirty television specials, and four feature films.

Charles Schulz's definition of happiness in this life was defined as "warm puppies, piles of leaves, finding the little puzzle piece with the pink edge and part of the sky and the top of the sailboat, and a piece of fudge caught on the first bounce."

Before his death in February 2000, Charles Schulz was still single-handedly creating every day, from his heart and soul, endearing snippets of everyday life that will be enjoyed for generations.

Your life is a wealth of creative potential. Someone once said, "Each of us who dares to reach in and pull out what is truly ourselves brings a new way of seeing into the world."

Getting in touch with your own unique and authentic self releases creativity that can only come from your journey and life experiences. Create means to bring into being, to give rise to. No one can tell your story, write your songs or poetry, paint a flower, or give life to thoughts and ideas in the same way that you can! The word *creative* is defined as "inventive, imaginative." It is your creative perspective that may

allow someone to hear, see, or grasp the meaning of something for the first time.

Creativity is alive in you because the Creator of life instilled it in you. You were born to be creative! It's like electricity—powerfully able to bring light and meet specific needs. And history books prove that age does not hinder the flow of creativity. At age seventy-nine, Oliver Wendell Holmes wrote Over the Teacups. *Tennyson wrote "Crossing the Bar" at age eighty-three. Goethe completed* Faust *at eighty. Verdi, at eighty-five, composed his famous "Ave Maria."*

Author John Leax said that "writing is aligning his

CREATIVITY

personal will with the will of God, becoming a person in whom God speaks." The same can be said of any creative gift God has given you.

Through creativity, you discover your deepest self and creative core that connects you with the Creator of all. Expressing what makes your heart rejoice or your soul weep allows God, through you, to bring sacred light to others.

If you are in Christ, you are a new creation! You are the work of My hands, specifically designed to creatively contribute to the good works that I've prepared in advance just for you. I've gifted you to impact your corner of the world as only you can.

Inspiring you,

Your Creator and
Heavenly Father

2 Corinthians 5:17; Ephesians 2:10
1 Corinthians 7:7

I've gifted you…

COURAGE

It took a great deal of courage to put aside a novel she had started less than a year earlier, marry a man with three children, and establish a new home and family at age forty-four. But surprisingly, Catherine and her new husband, Leonard, made a great editorial team—she was the writer and he the editor. They spent wonderful times together plotting actions and developing characters for Catherine's books. Their working relationship became an integral part of their lives and even produced a coauthored book titled *My Personal Prayer Diary*.

Catherine's writing career did not begin easily. When her first husband, a chaplain for the U.S. Senate, died suddenly of a heart attack, she was left to raise their nine-year-old son alone. A short time later, Catherine began writing a biography of her brilliant and highly respected husband, which included some of his sermons and prayers. It was the first of more than

*Life is either a
daring adventure
or nothing. To
keep our faces
toward change
and behave like
free spirits in the
presence of fate
is strength
undefeatable.*

—HELEN KELLER

twenty books she would author during a span of the next thirty-four years.

Those closest to Catherine Marshall knew her as a woman intensely devoted in her desire for intimacy with Jesus Christ—and all who read Catherine's books were motivated to experience God in exciting new ways.

Through all of her personal trials—including the deaths of two of her own grandchildren in 1966 and 1971—and her own suffering of many years with debilitating emphysema, Catherine's steadfast courage and faith in God never wavered but instead drew her closer to the Master's heart.

Catherine's first novel—a story inspired by her own mother's journey to the Appalachian Mountains to teach impoverished children, took nine years to write and was published in 1967. Hailed as Catherine's biggest success, *Christy* also became a popular television series.

Julie, Catherine Marshall's nineteenth book, took seven years to write. It is based on her own memories of life in West Virginia when she was eighteen years old. Leonard LeSourd, Catherine's husband and editor of *Guidepost* magazine for twenty-eight years, stated, "In many ways *Julie* is Catherine's own story, because the passion for causes, the quest for faith and the courageous spirit in Julie Wallace were also in Catherine."

Before her death in 1983, Catherine Marshall's book sales totaled more than sixteen million copies. When Catherine's pen was stilled, her husband published Catherine's last book—writings from her personal journal titled *A Closer Walk*.

Catherine's inspirational words testify of her faith and courage and still speak to us today: "No matter how late the hour, no matter how desperate the moment, we cannot despair; the joy and the riches He has promised stretch like a shining road into the future."

43

You and I are not guaranteed smooth sailing through life's journey.

Clouds loom. Storms come.

And sometimes you feel you've been cast into a raging sea of uncertainty. In those moments you may wonder if the tide of despair will pull you under—or...if through the shadowy sea mist you'll see the promise of sunshine again, if dreams once dreamed will ever come to pass.

Don't lose hope! God has given you a promise: "Be of good courage, and he shall strengthen your heart, all ye that hope in the LORD" (Psalm 31:24).

That means you won't drown in fear or doubt. You possess the courage to withstand any storms life may bring, because He is your anchor of hope. You can toss the whys and what ifs overboard and be assured that as surely as the frightened disciples in the boat heard Jesus say, "Peace be still," that He is also riding in your vessel and will calm your restless sea.

True courage stems from faith in a God who supplies the strength you need for all life's challenges. And when He is your hope, anything is possible.

COURAGE

Courage is the bridge that will take you to higher ground!

Sure, it takes courage to dare to dream again! But one step—one day—one moment at a time, you can walk with overcoming faith, courage, and determination toward new opportunities and blessings.

Life is full of possibilities. And with each new dawn, you're given another chance to behold, believe, and launch the dreams within your heart.

Don't be surprised when you encounter trouble. As long as you are living, you have hope. Your body and your heart may fail, but I am your strength and your portion forever! Come to Me when you're tired and discouraged, and I will give you rest. Even in your old age and gray hair, I'll take care of you and provide your needs. You'll discover how good it is to be near to Me!

Encouraging you,

Your God of Refuge

John 16:33; Ecclesiastes 9:4
Psalm 73:26, 28; Matthew 11:28
Isaiah 46:4

I am your strength and your portion…

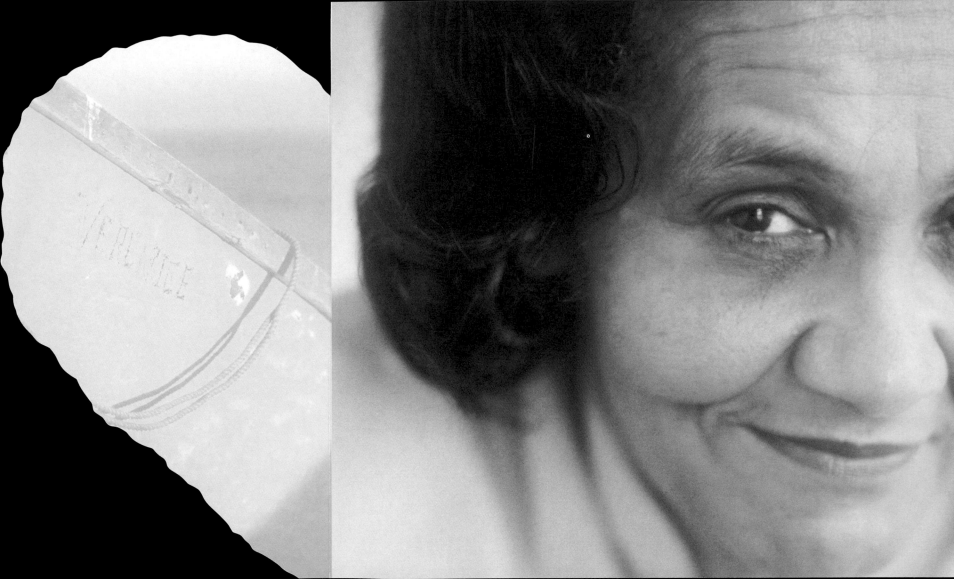

OPTIMISM

Still full of zest in his eighties, he is known as "the most believable voice in America" and embodies the spirit of the people he portrays on his program—hardworking, honest, and optimistic. He once said, "I've never seen a monument erected for a pessimist."

He's graced the Gallup Poll list of America's most admired men and received eleven honorary degrees, eleven Freedoms Foundation Awards, and has been named Commentator, Salesman, Person, Father, and American of the Year.

Paul and "Angel" (as he affectionately calls his wife) have been married for more than fifty years and still have the car they sat in when Paul proposed on their first date. The sentimental Nash Lafayette sits in a special garage, built on their 260-acre ranch in Missouri.

During his childhood Paul loved making homemade radios in cigar boxes with crystals and copper wire. Eventually, he hung around a local radio station so often that they finally hired him. His jobs included

I shall grow old, but never lose life's zest, because the road's last turn will be the best.

—HENRY VAN DYKE

everything from sweeping, playing the guitar, and announcing.

Paul began his daily newscasts from Chicago in 1944. His syndicated commentaries were aired nationally, starting in 1951 when the ABC network brought him to the nation.

Today, with more than twenty million listeners, Paul Harvey holds the world's largest communications conglomerate with thirteen hundred radio stations, four hundred stations on the American Forces Network, one hundred television stations, and three hundred newspapers. He has been elected to the National Association of Broadcasters Radio Hall of Fame and the Oklahoma Hall of Fame.

Descended from Baptist preachers, Paul's colorful writing style and broadcasts set him apart from his contemporaries. He explains things, he says, "in dime-store words."

Paul Harvey says the most newsworthy thing he ever reported was the birth of his son. He also believes "in leaving the woodpile a little higher than I found it."

His quote, "Like what you do; if you don't like it, *do something else*," reflects Paul Harvey's attitude and optimism toward life. While some believe in retiring at a certain age, Paul's work is his passion, and he plans to remain in broadcasting until he discovers something he loves more.

Paul Harvey enjoys spending time on his ranch, traveling, and being a car buff, but he once stated in an interview, "I find it very difficult to tell myself I ought to be sitting on a creek bank drowning worms, or I ought to be out there playing golf (the way I play golf) when I honestly would rather be sitting at that typewriter painting pictures."

That's why we still enjoy Paul Harvey's unique blend of hard news and homespun wit. The news stories that continue to profoundly impact the lives in America come from a man who confirms that "there is no age to the spirit" and that we can always look forward to…the rest of the story.

Do you know someone whose enthusiasm brightens your day and your outlook on life? Such people know how to look for the best—the greater good in every situation—believing that something great is on the horizon of every tomorrow.

You, too, can learn to look for tomorrow's horizon and see life as a great adventure, trusting that God has wonderful surprises in store for you! Being aware and interested in everyone and everything around you means you'll never quit learning and growing. You can welcome every season of life with wisdom—knowing that each holds its own gift, its own beauty and message.

An optimistic outlook fills you with a sense of awe at every bend of life's road.

From the long season of isolation beneath winter's cold earth, tulips and daffodils burst into spring bloom and are watered with the fresh rain of promise.

Summer brings spontaneous moments to walk barefoot in the grass and savor simple pleasures—like the taste of homemade ice cream or plucking wild blackberries. This exuberant season reminds us that God is the creator of abundance and that in Him there is no lack.

The rustling of autumn leaves brings forth a stirring

OPTIMISM

in your soul. Crisp breezes magically transform green leaves into gold-and-russet splendor as they dance to the melody of change.

Winter, when all seems silent and still, is a time of unseen renewal. Like the bulbs beneath the ground, you are called to rest and plan for spring's return.

Seasons are a beautiful sampling of God's infinite creativity and parables for living optimistically throughout the seasons of your life. Emily Dickinson's pen has well-defined optimism: "The mere sense of living is joy enough."

Learn the secret of being content in all situations. I'll satisfy you in the morning with My everlasting love, that you may sing for joy and be glad every day. Cheerfulness gives your heart reservations for a continual feast that supersedes your circumstances. The path of the righteous shines brighter and brighter with each day.

Love,

Your God of Abundant Life

Philippians 4:12; Psalm 90:14
Proverbs 15:15; 4:18

I'll satisfy you in the morning…

Dedication

I lovingly dedicate this book to my mom, Cora—the most "young at heart" person I've ever known. She's packed a lot of living into eighty-one years and still amazes everyone with her charm, vitality, and outlook on life. Mom raised nine children and has survived the ups and downs of life with wit, wisdom, and faith in God. Gifted with a "green thumb," she still grows enough vegetables and flowers each year to share with neighbors and anyone who comes to visit.

I thank God for blessing me with a mother who demonstrates every quality the themes in this book depict—insight, graciousness, faithfulness, servanthood, creativity, courage, and possibly her strongest quality of all…optimism.

The timeless truths my mom instilled in me continue to steady my steps throughout life's journey. From childhood she taught me to put God first and trust Him to work out everything in my life, that every cloud has a silver lining, and that treating others with kindness will make my own heart smile. Because of Mom's assurance that with God's help I could accomplish whatever I set my heart to do and that dreams really can come true, I'm living a few of those dreams today.

So, with a humble heart I honor my Mom—who has always said, "Give me my flowers while I'm living"—with this bouquet of thoughts and love.

Sources

Many sources were used in compiling the biographical sketches in this book. The following sources were primary.

Anna Mary Robertson
   Armstrong, William Howard. *Barefoot in the Grass: The Story of Grandma Moses*. Garden City, N.Y.: Doubleday Publishers, 1970.

Fred Rogers
   Zoba, Wendy Murray, "Won't You Be My Neighbor?" *Christianity Today*, vol. 44, 2000.
   Roe, Claudia. "Some Things Never Change, and Thank Heavens Mr. Rogers Is One of Them," *Biography*, vol. 4, issue 3, March 2000, 102.

Corrie ten Boom
   Stamps, Ellen de Kroon. *My Years with Corrie*. Old Tappan, N.J.: Fleming H. Revel, 1978.
   ten Boom, Corrie, and John and Elizabeth Sherrill, *The Hiding Place*. New York: Bantam/Fleming H. Revel, 1971.

Jimmy Carter
   Ariail, Dan, and Cheryl Heckler Feltz. *The Carpenter's Apprentice: The Spiritual Biography of Jimmy Carter*. Grand Rapids, Mich.: Zondervan Publishing House, 1996.

Sources

Charles Schulz
> Johnson, Rheta Grimsley. *Good Grief: The Story of Charles M. Schulz*. Kansas City: Andrews and McMeel, 1995.

Catherine Marshall
> Marshall, Catherine. *Julie*. Carmel, N.Y.: Avon Books, 1985.
> Orange County Public Library, Florida: www.ocls.lib.fl.us/

Paul Harvey
> Oklahoma State University Library: http://www.library.okstate.edu/about/awards/winners/harvey.htm.
> Biography Online-Cambridge Encyclopedia Database, © 1995 Cambridge University Press: www.biography.com.

Special Thanks

to my loving, supportive, and patient husband—Harvey Duke. Thanks to Marla Slough and Kelly Ramsey for research assistance. I also extend my gratitude to LeAnn Weiss, Philis Boultinghouse, Bob Kelly, Tammy Anderson, John Howard, and all of my friends at Howard Publishing.

Books coauthored by Susan Duke:

Heartlifters for Mom
Heartlifters for Friends
Heartlifters for Women
Heartlifters for Hope and Joy
Heartlifters for Teachers

Other great gift books from Howard Publishing:

Heartlifters for Mom
Heartlifters for Friends
Heartlifters for Women
Heartlifters for Hope and Joy
Heartlifters for Teachers
Hugs for Friends
Hugs for Dad
Hugs for Kids
Hugs for Mom
Hugs for Sisters
Hugs for Women
Hugs for Teachers

Hugs for Those in Love
Hugs for Grandparents
Hugs for the Holidays
Hugs for the Hurting
Hugs to Encourage and Inspire
Hugs for Grads
Hugs for Grandma
Hugs from Heaven: Embraced by the Savior
Hugs from Heaven: On Angel Wings
Hugs from Heaven: The Christmas Story
Hugs from Heaven: Celebrating Friendship
Hugs from Heaven: Portraits of a Woman's Faith